50 Fabulous Measurement Activities

Hands-On Activities for Exploring Length, Perimeter, Weight, Volume, and Time That Will Send Kids' Measurement Skills Sky High!

by Martin Lee and Marcia Miller

SCHOLASTIC
PROFESSIONAL BOOKS

NEW YORK • TORONTO • LONDON • AUCKLAND • SYDNEY
MEXICO CITY • NEW DELHI • HONG KONG

For Sasha and Avery—
great kids by any measure!

Cover design by Norma Ortiz
Cover photos by Donnelly Marks
Interior illustrations by James Graham Hale
Interior design by Solutions by Design, Inc.

ISBN: 0-590-64406-8

Contents

Dear Teacher,

Let's face it—measurement is messy.

Hands-on activities, by their very nature, can get messy and measurement is 100% hands-on. That's one reason some of us downplay measurement—and, of course, the reason most children love it! This book doesn't promise to do away with the messiness of good child-centered activities. But it does promise to suggest ways to immerse children in measurement, to involve them in estimating, calculating, doing, learning, internalizing, and taking control of this most hands-on of all math strands.

The National Council of Teachers of Mathematics (NCTM) recognizes the importance of including measurement activities in a complete curriculum. To paraphrase Standard 10 in *Curriculum and Evaluation Standards for School Mathematics:*

> Measurement activities help children understand the attributes of length, capacity, weight, area, and time [among others], develop measuring skill and familiarity with units of measure, estimate when measuring, and make and use measurements in varied situations.

That's just what we hope *50 Fabulous Measurement Activities* offers. Kids act like true mathematicians when they explore, question, guess, adjust, try again, and, finally, draw conclusions and make generalizations about measurement concepts and applications. Strong measurement skills will serve students well throughout their academic lives. Key measurement ideas support their understanding of number theory, data collection and analysis, geometry, fractions and decimals, and many topics in science.

Rich activities and investigations can also show children some of the ways that measurement fits into their daily lives. We believe that it's crucial to give kids the tools they need to tackle both the routine and the challenging measurement tasks we face day to day, as well as the language and experience they need to communicate mathematical ideas.

In some classrooms, measurement lessons tend to focus on helping children learn various equivalencies, such as 4 cups = 1 quart, or 60 seconds = 1 minute. Indeed, these facts are important and necessary, but memorizing them isn't the whole show. Children must experience measurement. They need to stretch their arms to show one yard, hold a one-pound bag of rice to know what a pound feels like, or balance on one foot for 30 seconds to understand how *very* long a half-minute can be!

This is the active approach that our book encourages. We hope that you and your class will enjoy it.

Merry measuring!

Marty Lee & Marcia Miller

About Measurement

What is measurement, and why should children study it?

Measurement is a process of determining the extent, size, number, capacity, temperature, duration, or other attribute that allows for quantification and comparison. Measurement allows children to predict and compare. It makes the world and the objects in it real, tangible, and countable.

How do children learn about measurement?

Developmentally, children move through three broad stages in their grasp of measurement.

☆ First, they engage in basic comparisons, such as "I'm older than Steve" or "Mom is taller than my teacher." Units of measure are irrelevant at this stage.

☆ Next, they explore indirect comparisons. For instance, they learn to express the distance across a room in numbers of footsteps. Or they sense what it means to stay up until a TV program ends. At this stage, nonstandard units come into play.

☆ Last, they begin to recognize the importance of being able to express measurement ideas to others, and to understand what others say about measurement to them. Also, they begin to demand greater precision and expect to be able to replicate results. Now it's time for standard units of measure for clarity, predictability, and exactness.

What kinds of measurement matter most?

A trick question! It depends on what you need to know. If you were building a cage for a giraffe, it wouldn't be enough to know the animal's height. If you wanted to know whether it was safe to dive into a swimming pool, it wouldn't help you to know the pool's perimeter or shape.

An object can be measured in many different ways, due to the breadth of measurement concepts. Suppose you want to express the measure of a shoe box. You might ask:

☆ How much does it hold? (capacity)

☆ How tall is it? (height)

☆ How long is it? (length)

☆ How deep is it? (depth)

☆ How heavy is it? (weight)

☆ How far is it around the outside? (perimeter)

☆ How much space does it cover on your closet floor? (area)

☆ How much room does it take up in your closet? (volume)

☆ How much paper would I need to wrap it? (surface area)

Clearly, a simple question can raise a series of valid—even complicated—measurement issues. *50 Fabulous Measurement Activities* can help set the tone for how children approach measurement in your classroom by inspiring questions, curiosity, and the desire to find and share answers.

About This Book

This book is divided into five parts. Parts 1–4 address separate topics of measurement: Length/Perimeter/Area, Weight, Capacity, and Time. These sections end with "Quickies"—kernels of ideas that you can turn into full-blown activities. Part 5 presents an array of activities that combine topics through surveys, games, events, and puzzles you can use to assess, summarize, or culminate the study of measurement. Pages 63–64 list suggested books related to each topic as well as some fun facts (courtesy of *The Guinness Book of Records*) you can use as springboards for discussion.

Each activity in this book begins by asking a question. You can pose this question directly to children to get their minds warmed up and their curiosity jump-started. Then you'll find an easy-to-follow lesson plan for helping children understand, analyze, and answer the question. Each activity has follow-up ideas—extensions, variations, discussion points, or challenges that arise from the original activity.

Teaching Tips

☆ Move through the book as you see fit. Within each part, activities appear in ascending order of complexity. Choose activities that fit your students' interests and skill level and adapt them to meet the needs of your students, your schedule, and your classroom closet.

☆ Set up a Measurement Station in your classroom. Stock it with assorted measuring tools, such as rulers, tape measures, yardsticks, string, trundle wheels, assorted containers, cups, clocks or stopwatches, balance scales, weights, and thermometers. Don't forget to include assorted objects to use as nonstandard units of measure, such as snap cubes, color tiles, lima beans, paper clips, index cards, grid paper, and so on.

☆ Take advantage of any measurement activities that arise in the natural course of your school day. Talk about them and work them out together.

☆ In this book, most activities that call for standard units of measure use customary ones. Feel free to recast any activity to make it work with metric units.

☆ Invite children to work on any of the activities at home with family members.

☆ Be a role model by showing that you, too, use measurement. Participate with the children: Estimate, measure, and share your creative and guiding ideas.

Individual Measuring Units

What part of you makes a good unit of measure?

Measuring was first done with nonstandard units: hand spans, arm lengths, paces, feet (the kind with toes!), and so on. Encourage children to explore measuring with personal units.

The Plan

1 Explain to children that nowadays we can measure lengths in units such as inches, feet, meters, or centimeters. By using standard units that everyone knows, we can agree what a certain length means. But long ago, people measured with what they had at hand— like their hands!

2 Write the initials IMU on the board. Tell children that it stands for Individual Measuring Unit. Challenge them to think about how to use their own bodies as measuring tools and choose a useful unit they can measure with. Examples might include the hand span, the length of a finger, the width of a fist, their "wingspan," the length from elbow to wrist, and so on.

3 Have children identify and describe their individual IMU and then use it to find the lengths of assorted classroom objects. Provide each child with a simple recording chart such as this one:

> ### MATERIALS
> ☆ various classroom objects
> ☆ recording chart (see below)
> ☆ pencils

My IMU: the distance between the tips of my thumb and index finger	
Object	Length in IMUs
Distance across my desk	4

Follow-Up

☆ Talk about the results of this investigation. Invite children to describe their IMUs and share some of the measurements they found.

☆ Rank IMUs from shortest to longest, or from easiest to trickiest to use.

☆ Discuss questions such as these: *Are any IMUs the same? Did any students measure the same object? What happened? What conclusions can we draw about the value of having standard measures?*

Stepping Out

How can you get a feeling for greater distances?

It's not that hard for children to learn to visualize an inch, a foot, a yard, or a meter. It's trickier for them to grasp even greater distances. This "feet-on" activity will help.

The Plan

1 Ask a volunteer to demonstrate the "giant step" (a full-length stride). Ask the class to estimate how many giant steps they think it would take to cross the classroom. Record children's guesses, then have several volunteers step it out to verify the estimates. Repeat the question, this time with a different distance, such as the length from the front of the room to the back or from the chalkboard to the pencil sharpener. Again, record estimates, and then have children step it out. (Explain to students that since a giant step is not a standard unit of measurement, their answers will vary.)

> **MATERIALS**
> ☆ recording chart (see below)
> ☆ pencils

2 When children become better estimators of greater distances, take them outside, as weather permits, or to a large indoor area, such as the cafeteria, gym, or a school corridor. Pose the same estimation question: *How many giant steps would it take you to get from here to there?* Have children work with partners to record their estimates on a simple chart like the one shown and then step it out to find it out. Repeat with various distances, long and longer!

From—	To—	Estimated Giant Steps	Actual Giant Steps

3 Back in the classroom, tell children that the distance we call a mile came from an old Roman unit of measure. The Roman mile was marked by 1000 double-steps (like giant steps). Using this as a benchmark, challenge children to estimate about how far, in miles or parts of a mile, they would need to walk to go from one landmark to another on the school grounds. On a nice day, you might want to have children check their estimates for some of the shorter distances.

Follow-Up

☆ If possible, obtain a pedometer or trundle wheel. Help children experiment with these tools to measure greater distances.

☆ Arrange a trip to a local golf course or driving range (when no one is hitting!), where greater distances are marked. Have children compare their giant steps with standard distances.

Inching Along

How can you improve your eye for inches?

The inch is an important measure in children's daily lives. This activity will help familiarize them with inches and sharpen their eyes for lengths in inches.

The Plan

1 Give children inch rulers to examine. Tell them that you want them to try to fix the size of 1 inch in their minds. After a few moments, ask them to put the rulers away. Now challenge them to draw a line that is 1 inch long. Have them compare their line to 1 inch on the ruler. How many students drew lines that were too long? Too short? Pretty close? Try again. What changes do children notice?

2 Now ask children to study how long 6 inches is on the ruler. Then have them put the ruler aside, try to draw a 6-inch line by hand, and then check it for accuracy. Repeat several times to help children sharpen their "inch sense."

3 Finally, ask children, without getting up, to scan the classroom to identify six objects they guess to be about 6 inches long. Have them list the objects in a chart like the one shown. Then have them use rulers to check their predictions. They record actual lengths in inches and rate the chosen objects as longer than, shorter than, or exactly 6 inches.

MATERIALS
☆ inch rulers
☆ recording chart (see below)
☆ various classroom objects
☆ pencils

Object	Actual Length	Longer?	Shorter?	Exactly?
stapler	7"	✔		

Follow-Up

☆ Try similar investigations with different lengths: 2 inches, 4 inches, 8 inches, and so on.

☆ Challenge children to find a set of objects that represent 1-, 2-, 3-, 4-, and 5-inch lengths.

☆ Have children discover personal benchmarks that are equivalent to an inch, such as the length of the first joint of the index finger, the width of two fingers, a thumbprint, and so on.

"Inch by Inch" Game

How well can you judge the lengths of lines?

Games provide a motivating way for kids to practice measurement skills in a high-interest setting. This simple card game reinforces recognizing lengths to 6 inches.

The Plan

1 In advance, prepare two game decks as follows:

☆ 12 number cards, two of each with the numbers 1, 2, 3, 4, 5, and 6.

☆ 12 line cards, on which you draw unlabeled 1-, 2-, 3-, 4-, 5-, and 6-inch lines, two cards for each length. Give each segment end marks for clarity of measuring.

2 Mix together each deck, then place them face-down with number cards in one pile, line cards in another.

3 Form groups of three to six children. Each group needs a scorekeeper and a judge to verify lengths with a ruler. These jobs can rotate during the game.

4 To play, the first child turns over one number card and one line card for all to see. If the player thinks that the pair matches—that is, if the number gives the length of the line—the child says, "Match." If the child believes that the cards do not match, he or she says, "No match." Either way, the judge then measures the line to verify the guess. A correct guess earns 2 points. An incorrect guess earns 1 point.

5 Remix the decks frequently. Play continues in turn until someone earns 7 points.

MATERIALS

☆ 4- x 6-inch index cards (or construction paper)
☆ inch rulers
☆ paper and pencils

Follow-Up

☆ Create variations of the game to match the measurement skills of your class. For example, children who are adept at measuring and estimating to the nearest half-inch can use a deck of cards with lengths that challenge this skill.

☆ Use the same deck to play "Inch by Inch" Concentration. Using the rules of that old favorite game, children can turn over two cards at a time to look for pairs. A pair consists of a number card and a line card that match (not two cards with the same number or two cards with the same length lines). Keep a ruler handy for judging.

Body Geometry

What are you—a rectangle or a square?

You'd never picture anyone in your class as being a rectangle or a square, but heights and widths can tell a geometric story! Try this investigation to learn how.

The Plan

1 Review the definitions of squares and rectangles. (Use this age-appropriate definition: Both are four-sided figures with square corners. All sides of a square are of equal length. A rectangle has two longer sides and two shorter sides; opposite sides are equal.)

2 Ask a volunteer to stand tall with both arms fully extended at shoulder height, parallel to the floor. Ask the other children to imagine drawing a big box around the outside of the person. Would that box be a rectangle or a square? How can we tell?

3 Provide string, scissors, and masking tape. Have children work in pairs to help each other take two string measurements: one that shows full height, the other that shows full arm extension (fingertip to fingertip), or wingspan. HINT: It may be easier for kids being measured to lie on the floor. Children cut two lengths of string for each person and attach a masking tape label that says "H" for height or "W" for width.

4 Have children compare the lengths of their height strings and wingspan strings. If height and wingspan are the same length, that person is a square! If one string is longer than the other, that person is a rectangle.

5 Provide paper squares and rectangles on which children write their names to show which shape matches their body dimensions.

MATERIALS
- ☆ string
- ☆ scissors
- ☆ masking tape
- ☆ 2-inch paper squares and 2- x 4-inch rectangles
- ☆ chart paper (or bulletin board space)
- ☆ markers

Follow-Up

☆ Have students use actual measurements to record their body lengths and widths.

☆ Are grown-ups rectangles or squares? How about animals? Have children extend this exploration at home by measuring the height and wingspan of family members, including pets!

Feet of Feet

How many feet of feet are there in our class?

Long ago, the measure known as a foot equaled the length of the royal foot. For each new king or queen, the unit changed! Feet now, like feet then, still come in all sizes. Why not have children figure out how many feet of feet they have in all?

The Plan

Talk about ways to measure the length of a foot. For instance, will children measure bare feet, or will shoes and/or socks stay on? Will they measure feet as a person stands on them or as the person sits? Will this matter?

> **MATERIALS**
> ☆ inch rulers or tape measures
> ☆ calculator
> ☆ chart paper
> ☆ markers

Pick a plan, then decide how to proceed. Try one or more of these methods:

1 Have children find the length of each of their feet in inches, then find the sum of the two lengths in inches. List each child's total foot length. Then calculate the class total in inches.

2 Divide the class into small groups. Children in each group stand in line, one foot ahead of the other, heel to toe. Ask another child to measure the total length of all the feet in the group. Combine group totals for the class total.

3 Have the whole class stand in line, heel to toe, as volunteers measure the total length of all feet. Don't forget to add the foot lengths of the measurers!

4 Make a heel-to-toe chain of water footprints on an outdoor sidewalk. Don't leave space between footprints, and work quickly before the prints dry. Measure the total length of the chain of footprints.

5 Use a calculator to divide the inch total by 12 to express the total length in feet.

Follow-Up

☆ Repeat this activity later in the year, after children have grown some. Predict the change in the total length, then measure to find out.

☆ Find out how feet in your classroom compare to the standard foot. Whose feet are exactly 1 foot long? More than a foot long? Less than a foot long? Graph this data.

How Far Is the Flick?

How good are you at estimating short distances?

Children can become better estimators, but it won't happen in a flicker of time. Try this investigation to see that practice makes perfect. Well, it makes for improvement anyway!

The Plan

1 Choose an open area in the classroom that all children can see. From a marked starting point, flick a coin. Ask children to estimate the length of the flick. Record the guesses. Then ask a volunteer to use a ruler to measure the actual length in feet and inches. Record that distance. How close was the estimate?

2 Divide the class into small groups and tell children that they are going to flick an object, estimate how far it has gone, and then find the actual distance. Provide each group with small disks to flick. Demonstrate how to use the middle finger and thumb to flick. Invite children to practice this technique.

SAFETY NOTE: Discuss with children the importance of flicking objects into an open space and not in the direction of their classmates or teacher.

3 Then find or create other open areas in your classroom, or move to the hall or to an empty room in which coins won't end up in a fish tank or paint pot. Have children use tape to mark starting lines from which to flick. Distribute copies of a table like this one.

Flick	Estimate	Actual Measurement
1		
2		
3		
4		

4 In turn, children flick an object. They and others in their group estimate how far it has gone, recording the estimates in their tables. Then they measure and record the actual distance. Have children repeat this process four or more times.

Follow-Up

☆ Talk about the results. Were children's estimates close? Were they generally too high or too low? Did they improve with practice?

MATERIALS

☆ small "flickable" disks (such as coins or checkers)

☆ rulers

☆ tape

☆ recording table (see below)

☆ markers

Creative Closet

In how many ways can you measure an article of clothing?

Clothing manufacturers make shopping easier with standard sizes for garments. Once shoppers know their neck size, waist measure, sleeve length, and so on, they know just where to look on shelves and racks for clothes that fit. But there are other, creative ways to measure what we wear.

The Plan

1 Bring in several old garments of various sizes.

2 Divide the class into small groups of two to four children and give each group an article of clothing.

3 Have them look at the label and tell classmates what size it is. Then tell children that 8, 10, or 12, or small, medium, or large, aren't the only ways to identify the size of a garment. Another approach to describing how big an article of clothing is might be to measure its features. What is the length of a sleeve? The length of a zipper? The width of a pocket?

> **MATERIALS**
> ☆ jackets, coats, sweats, and other outer garments
> ☆ tape measures or rulers
> ☆ pencils
> ☆ 4- x 6-inch index cards
> ☆ paper clips

4 Brainstorm with children a list of imaginative ways to measure outerwear. Have them carefully examine their articles anew to spark ideas. If children are stumped, suggest some measurements to jumpstart their creativity. Mention, for instance, the size of collars or cuffs, the size of buttons or the distance between them, the length of drawstrings, the depth of pockets, or width of stripes.

5 Once children have established their own unique set of measurements, distribute tape measures or rulers, pencils, and index cards and have them make those measurements (in inches or centimeters). Then have them transfer their measurements onto an index card, which will become a new clothing tag. When they finish, they can clip the tag onto the garment.

6 Invite children to present their newly measured outerwear to the other "shoppers" in the class. Guide them to point out and describe the many "sizes" of their coat, jacket, sweatshirt, or sweater. Remind them also to mention the garment's other, more traditional features, such as what material it's made of and what color it is.

Follow-Up

☆ Compile class data on the new measurements. Guide children to examine those that appear on several children's tags (distance between buttons, depth of pockets, length of zipper, for instance). Is there any uniformity?

Estimating Spirals

How can you draw a spiral that's a foot long?

Tell children that if you asked them to draw a straight line that's 1 foot long, they would, after a few tries and measurement checks, get pretty good at it. (Try it and see!) But how good are their estimating skills when it comes to drawing a spiral that's 1 foot long?

The Plan

1 Draw a spiral like the one below on blank paper. Draw it as a continuous line, approximately 1 yard long, without lifting your pencil. Display the spiral for all to see. Ask children to guess how long the line is. Record their guesses.

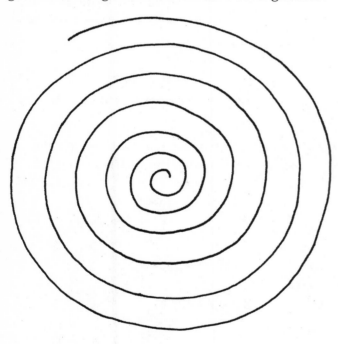

2 Ask children to explain how they would go about measuring the actual length of the line. As needed, guide them to see that a sensible way is to lay string along the spiraling path and then straighten out the string and measure its

MATERIALS
- ☆ blank paper
- ☆ rulers or tape measures
- ☆ string
- ☆ pencils

length with a ruler. After children have measured their spirals this way, ask if any guesses were close. How close were they?

3 Distribute blank sheets of paper, pencils, rulers, and string. Challenge children to make a spiral that is 1 foot long. Then ask them to use string to measure the actual length of their line and to record it. How close were they?

4 Now have children try to draw another 1-foot spiral, measure it, and then draw a third. After children have drawn their spirals, measured all three, and recorded their measurements, ask them to describe the results. Do estimates improve with practice?

5 When you think children are getting pretty good at drawing 1-foot spirals, challenge them to draw a spiral that's 1 yard long.

Follow-Up

☆ Have a class art exhibition with one special feature: All works of art must be line drawings of animals, and all drawings must consist of a continuous line that's about 1 yard long. (No snakes or worms!) Display artists' work for all to admire.

Map Sense

What measurement units would you use to map parts of the neighborhood?

Visual thinking is at the heart of mapmaking. In this mapping activity, children have to choose sensible measurement units to use for each item they include on a map.

The Plan

1 Ask children to tell how they would go about drawing a map of a part of their neighborhood (or school grounds, cafeteria, or playground, as appropriate). You may find it useful to show them some examples of very simple maps or schematic drawings.

2 Distribute paper, pencils, rulers, and clipboards, and take children on a walking tour of the area they will map. Instruct them to sketch or take notes on what they see to help them remember details for their maps. Or allow children to sketch their maps on-site. Emphasize that they should keep in mind how big each thing is in comparison to other things around it.

3 Have children make their maps. Tell them to name each item they include and to label it with the unit they would use to measure it. For example, they might label a fire hydrant "feet" or "feet and inches." A house might have the label "yards." Children should give their maps a descriptive title.

4 Post children's maps or bind them to create a class atlas.

MATERIALS
☆ rulers
☆ pencils or markers
☆ clipboard (or other hard surface for writing)

Follow-Up

☆ Have children make simple maps of their street or of a place they have visited, such as a zoo, sports arena, shopping mall, or theme park.

Hands Down, Kites Up!

How can you measure the size of your hand?

A hand-tracing activity that results in a "hands-on" graph will help students explore the concept of perimeter—and it's sure to win their applause.

The Plan

(1) Provide pairs of children with construction paper, pencils, string, scissors, and tape. Tell them that they are going to find out the distance around their hands.

(2) Instruct one partner to place his or her hand, palm down, on the paper, fingers spread wide apart to make the hand easy to trace. Ask the other partner to carefully trace the outline of the hand in pencil. Partners then switch roles so that each has an outlined hand. Have children write their name within their hand outline.

(3) Have partners work together to place the string carefully on the traced outlines. They can also tape the string in place. Demonstrate these methods.

(4) Have children cut the string (removing the tape as needed). Then they should straighten the string out to its full length and measure it.

(5) Next, ask children to cut out their labeled hand shape. Have them tape or staple their length of string to the bottom of the cut-out hand to create, in effect, a hand-shaped kite.

(6) Help children display their handkites to create a concrete horizontal graph of class hand sizes.

MATERIALS
- ☆ construction paper
- ☆ pencils
- ☆ string or yarn
- ☆ scissors
- ☆ tape or stapler

Follow-Up

☆ Have children arrange the handkite graph to show hand sizes in ascending or descending order. Ask them to write in their math journals a summary of what the graph shows about their classmates' hand sizes.

☆ Try a similar investigation with feet (the kind with toes).

Area Cover-Up

How many nonstandard units cover a region?

This activity challenges children to use nonstandard units to cover a surface. They will face the problem of what to do when the units they use do not cover the region exactly.

The Plan

1 Have pairs of children clear the surface of their desks or tables. Or clear rectangular areas on the classroom floor for them to measure, and mark them off with masking tape. Distribute index cards (or other nonstandard measurement units). Tell children that they will use these cards to measure the size of the surface of their desk (or table or floor).

2 First ask children to predict how many cards they will need to completely cover the desk—no overlapping or going past the edge. Have them record that number.

3 Then have them find out how many it actually will take by placing cards on the surface until it is completely covered.

4 Guide pairs to think about the following questions as they work:

☆ *How do we place the cards—in any order? In organized rows?*

☆ *Do we place them vertically or horizontally?*

☆ *How do we account for leftover places too small for a card?*

5 After children have completed their measurements, have them report their findings. Ask them not only to tell how many cards covered their desks but also to explain the method they used. Ask them to explain how they dealt with leftover spaces. Have them compare their actual measurements with their estimates.

6 Have pairs repeat the activity, this time using a different nonstandard unit of measure. Make sure they estimate before measuring.

> **MATERIALS**
> ☆ nonstandard rectangular units to measure area (index cards, playing cards, sheets of paper, paper napkins, and so on)
> ☆ paper and pencils

Follow-Up

☆ Challenge groups to estimate and then measure to find out how many math textbooks will completely cover the classroom floor or how many sheets of paper will completely cover a bulletin board. HINT: Guide children to realize that they can measure about half the surface, then double that number to find the number needed to cover the entire surface.

Value of Money

How many coins are equal—in size—to a one-dollar bill?

Your students are likely to know that 100 pennies, 10 dimes, 20 nickels, and 4 quarters are all equal in value to one dollar. But are they equal in size as well? Do the following activity to learn about another, albeit unconventional, way of sizing up the value of a dollar in coins.

The Plan

1 Review the monetary relationships between a dollar and the number of pennies, nickels, dimes, and quarters equal to it. Then ask: *About how many of each of these coins will fit on a dollar bill, with no overlapping and no spilling over the edges? What do you think will be worth more—a dollar full of pennies, nickels, dimes, or quarters?* (The answer would be quarters, worth four dollars.) Tell them that they are going to find out.

2 Distribute play money to groups. Have children make a recording chart like this one:

$1 holds

ONE CENT	FIVE CENTS	ONE DIME	QUARTER DOL.
Guess:	Guess:	Guess:	Guess:
Actual:	Actual:	Actual:	Actual:
Value:	Value:	Value:	Value:

3 Tell children to first estimate how many pennies can fit on the bill without overlapping or going over any edges and record their guess. Then have them actually cover the bill with the

> **MATERIALS**
> ☆ play coins (pennies, nickels, dimes, quarters)
> ☆ play dollar bills
> ☆ rulers
> ☆ paper and pencils

pennies, count the exact number, and record the number on the table. Have them find the total value of the pennies on the dollar.

4 Repeat for the other coins: Estimate and record, cover and record, find the value and record. Do estimates "on the dollar" improve with each cover-up?

5 Have groups compare their results and methods. Ask them to explain how they arranged the coins on their dollar bill to fit the most they could. Have them share how their estimates measured up to the actual measurements.

Follow-Up

☆ Have students think of other areas to measure using the above procedure. How many coins do they think are needed to cover a sheet of notebook paper? How about a baseball card, a postcard, or a computer diskette?

Kiss 'n' Count

How can you describe the size of your kiss?

When you give someone a big kiss, what mathematical meaning does that smacker have? This activity will help children find out!

The Plan

1 Ask children: *How big is your biggest kiss?* After they giggle, most children will realize that they don't how to answer! Tell them that one way to measure the size of a kiss is to figure out how much space it covers.

2 Provide children with 4- x 6-inch pieces of light-colored construction paper. Demonstrate how to lightly coat the lips with lip gloss, vegetable oil, or petroleum jelly, and then kiss the paper as you press it to your lips. When you remove the paper, a kiss mark will remain. Trace its outline with a crayon. Help children do the same for their own kisses.

3 Provide dried beans that children can use as nonstandard units of measure. Have them cover the kiss with a single layer of beans. Encourage children to place the beans as close together as possible to cover up all the space inside the kiss without spilling over the outline.

4 When the kiss is completely filled, have children count the number of beans. This number reflects the size, or area, of the kiss in nonstandard units.

5 Record kiss areas in a line plot, bar graph, or other form of visual representation.

> ### MATERIALS
> ☆ construction paper
> ☆ lip gloss, vegetable oil, or petroleum jelly
> ☆ crayons
> ☆ dried beans with flat sides (lentils, split peas, and so on)

Follow-Up

☆ Try a similar investigation to determine the lip area of a frown, a pout, or a wide-open yell (silent, of course!).

☆ Find the area of a footprint with mini-marshmallows.

☆ Find the area of a handprint, using a thumbprint as the nonstandard unit of measure.

50 Fabulous Measurement Activities Scholastic Professional Books

All Square

What does a square foot really look like?

Many measurements of area that children might encounter in real life are expressed in square inches, square feet, square yards, or square meters. How well do children visualize these dimensions? After this activity, they'll do a lot better than before!

The Plan

1 Review the characteristics of a square (a figure with four equal sides and four square corners). Tell children that when we measure area, we express the measure in terms of square units—square inches, square feet, square yards, square miles, and so on.

2 Challenge children to draw a square that they think measures 1 inch on a side—a square inch. Do not let them use any measuring tools.

3 Ask them to look at each other's attempts and guess which square is closest to 1 square inch. Have children measure to find out. Then have each child use a ruler to draw a square inch.

4 Repeat, but now challenge children to use string, yarn, or tape to mark off a square they think covers 1 square foot. When they are satisfied, they should measure to test their guess and then use a ruler to mark a square foot. Repeat with 1 square yard. Or recast the activity so that children investigate 1 square centimeter, 1 square decimeter, and 1 square meter.

5 After children have a better sense of the size of these square units, have partners work together to fill in a chart similar to the one below. They should use the squares that they measured with a ruler to test how many different objects can fit within each square.

> **MATERIALS**
> ☆ paper and pencils
> ☆ string, yarn, or tape
> ☆ measuring tools (tape measures, rulers, meter sticks, and so on)
> ☆ recording chart (see below)

I square inch	I square foot	I square yard
2 peanuts	5 sneakers	

Follow-Up

☆ Challenge children to follow the same procedure to estimate other square areas, such as 4 square inches or 9 square feet.

☆ Go outside and have children work in teams to mark off greater square areas, such as 25 square feet or 16 square yards.

Quickies

Shadow Lengths

Have children measure the lengths of shadows at different times of day. They can measure shadows of trees, fence posts, or themselves (working in pairs). Have children record the lengths in standard or nonstandard units. Then compare lengths at different times of day to draw scientific conclusions.

Real-Life Perimeters

Take a walk around your school building to investigate its perimeter, using standard or nonstandard units (such as giant steps). Ask: *What shape is it? How many sides does it have? What is the length of each side? Which sides are longest? Shortest? Are any sides equal in length? What is its perimeter?* When they return to the classroom, have students draw a simple map of the results.

Squid Eyes!

According to the *Guinness Book of Records*, the giant squid has the largest eye of any living creature, modern or extinct! The giant squid's eye measures 15 $^3/_4$ inches across! Present this amazing fact to children and have them measure out 15 $^3/_4$ inches to get a sense of the size of a squid's eye. Then have partners carefully measure the width of each other's eyes and other body parts. Ask: *Who has the widest eye in your class? Who has the longest eyebrow? The biggest big toe? The smallest pinky toe? The longest hair? The tallest ear?* List some sizes to investigate, measure, chart, and marvel at!

Clay Play

Give each child a same-size blob of modeling clay, about the size of a plum. (Equalize the blobs: Weigh them, use a measuring cup, or form a cylinder from which you slice off equal chunks.) Have children work with the clay to form the longest possible "rope" they can without breaking apart the clay. Measure the clay ropes with tape measures, string, or rulers to determine which is longest. Graph or chart the results.

Weight Questionnaire

What objects are heavy? Which ones are light?

Before studying weight in terms of formal units of measure, such as ounces, pounds, tons, grams, or kilograms, children should first build weight sense. How? By classifying things as heavy, light, easy to lift, or too heavy to carry.

The Plan

1 Ask children what it means to ask how much something weighs (how heavy it is). Focus their thinking on weight by brainstorming a list of questions that have to do with comparing objects by weight. Here are some sample questions to get you started:

> ☆ Name something that weighs about the same as you do.
>
> ☆ Name five things that weigh less than you do.
>
> ☆ Name five things that weigh more than you do.
>
> ☆ Name five things that are too heavy for you to carry across the room.
>
> ☆ Name five things that are light enough to carry across the room with one finger.
>
> ☆ Name five things that are heavy but that you could lift for 10 seconds.
>
> ☆ Name four things you could carry if you had a friend to help.
>
> ☆ Name three things that even the strongest person you know could not carry.

MATERIALS
☆ chart paper
☆ pencils

2 Copy the best questions onto a questionnaire you can duplicate for children, or write them on the board. Have children work in pairs or groups to find sensible answers to the questions.

3 Share responses in a whole-class discussion. List children's ideas on chart paper. Encourage children to debate if they have very different responses.

Follow-Up

☆ Challenge children to examine similar questions at home with family members.

Weight Ranking

How can you decide which object is heavier?

Comparing weights is easy with objects of vastly different weights. But what happens if you want to compare objects that fall within a closer weight range? A balance scale can help.

The Plan

① Display two containers of the same size and shape—one that is empty and one that has some sand in it. Ask children to tell which is heavier. Most will say that the one holding sand weighs more. Have a volunteer test this assumption by lifting both containers.

② Prepare sets of three or four containers that have different amounts of sand or water in them. Divide the class into small groups. Challenge groups to rank containers from lightest to heaviest (or vice versa). Have them use their weight sense to determine the rankings.

③ When children have ranked the containers, provide a balance scale. Help them use it to test their findings and adjust their rankings as necessary.

④ Have children rotate to different groups to get more practice in weight comparisons.

MATERIALS
- ☆ closed containers holding sand or water
- ☆ balance scale (see page 29 for alternatives)
- ☆ various classroom objects

Follow-Up

☆ Prepare groups of five to seven objects. Have children work with partners or in small groups to rank the objects from lightest to heaviest (or vice versa). Challenge them by including two objects that are the same weight.

☆ For an extra challenge, narrow the weight range within the set of objects to make the task more difficult.

Twofers

Is it possible to balance one object with two others? With three others?

The balance scale is a great tool for problem solving as well as for weighing. In this activity, children use their senses of weight and balance to solve problems.

The Plan

1 Provide balance scales (or make simple balance boards) for this activity.

2 Demonstrate how to use the balance scale. Be sure that children recognize which side is heavier (lower) and which is lighter (higher).

3 Introduce the term *twofers*. Explain that it comes from the idea of getting two things for the price of one, such as two theatre tickets for the cost of one or two pieces of candy for one cent.

4 Have children work in pairs or small groups to create a series of "twofer equations" that show which two objects balance one object. For example, children might find that one chalkboard eraser balances two markers. Have them record their findings in a table like this one:

I	Balances	2
chalkboard eraser	balances	markers

> **MATERIALS**
> ☆ balance scales (see page 29 for alternatives)
> ☆ various classroom objects
> ☆ recording table (see below)
> ☆ pencils

5 Have children use the balance scale to develop at least five twofer equations.

Follow-Up

☆ Have children try a similar investigation with "three-fers" and "four-fers."

Around a Pound

What objects weigh more than a pound? Less than a pound?

An effective way for children to develop weight sense is to get a feel for some key weights. In this activity, children compare weights of objects to the benchmark of 1 pound.

The Plan

1 Write the term *benchmark* on the chalkboard. Tell children that a benchmark is a known measure or quantity that can be used to test and determine unknown quantities.

2 Review the inequality symbols < (is less than) and > (is greater than).

3 Prepare inequality floor mats for each group. You can make them from fabric (old towels, cut-up sheets, or tablecloths) or from craft paper, poster-board, or any other available material. Divide each mat into two columns. Label one column with the symbol for "is less than"(<) and the other with the symbol for "is greater than"(>).

< 1 pound	> 1 pound

4 Have children select any ten objects from the room. Then give each group a benchmark 1-pound weight to compare with the weights of the objects. Then ask children to sort the objects onto the appropriate side of the floor mat.

5 After children finish sorting their objects, talk about the benchmark estimating process and the choices they made. You may want to have them use a bathroom scale or other measuring instrument to verify their work and make any necessary adjustments.

> **MATERIALS**
> ☆ floor mats (see below)
> ☆ benchmark objects that weigh 1 pound (box of rice or pasta, canned pumpkin, ball of clay, and so on)
> ☆ various toys, books, or classroom objects
> ☆ bathroom scale or other weight measuring instrument (optional)

Follow-Up

☆ Try the same investigation with different benchmarks—for example, objects that weigh 8 ounces (1/2 pound), 5 pounds, or 1 kilogram.

Weight

How Many to a Pound?

What does a pound look like?

Well, that depends on the object! If a sign says that apples are 45¢ a pound, how many apples do you get for 45¢? Children can start to become smart shoppers by getting a sense of how many fruits or veggies make 1 pound.

The Plan

1 Have children hold a 1-pound weight and get a sense of how heavy it feels. Then ask them to estimate how many apples weigh 1 pound. Record their guesses. Then bring out some real apples and have a volunteer use the balance scale to answer the question.

2 Repeat with other items. Have children first guess and then verify their guesses using the balance scale and actual objects. Provide each child with a recording chart such as this one:

Item	GUESS How Many to a Pound?	ACTUAL Number to a Pound
apples		
bananas		

> **MATERIALS**
> ☆ balance scale
> ☆ 1-pound weights
> ☆ various foods (peanuts in the shell, apples, potatoes, onions, and so on)
> ☆ recording chart (see below)
> ☆ pencils

Follow-Up

☆ Encourage children to make generalizations about the number of items to the pound. Some may say that the heavier the item, the fewer you get in a pound. Others may notice that if items come in varied sizes, you might be able to mix and match them to get closer to exactly 1 pound.

☆ Talk with children about what happens in a store when someone wants to buy more or less than an exact pound. If possible, bring in grocery store receipts that show produce weighed by the pound and its price calculated accordingly.

Balancing Act

How can you use weights you know to find weights you don't know?

Before digital scales or spring scales, people used balance scales and fixed weights to find unknown weights. Obtain a balance scale and fixed weights so children can use this ancient technique to weigh modern objects.

The Plan

1 Display a balance scale and fixed weights. Talk about how to use these tools to weigh an object. Discuss that with this system, people can find approximate weights by discovering, for example, that an object is heavier than 1 pound but less than $1\frac{1}{2}$ pounds.

2 Demonstrate how to use different combinations of weights to determine more accurately the weight of an object. For example, if 8 ounces is too light but 1 pound is too heavy, show how to add 1-ounce weights to the 8-ounce weight until the pans balance.

3 Provide an assortment of objects for children to weigh as accurately as they can.

4 Monitor children as they work, suggesting ways to improve their approximations.

5 Show children how to record their findings in a table or on a chart.

6 Have different groups of children measure the same objects so that the class can compare strategies and findings.

> **MATERIALS**
> ☆ balance scale
> ☆ fixed weights (ounces, pounds, or grams)
> ☆ various objects to weigh
> ☆ chart paper
> ☆ pencils

Follow-Up

☆ As children gain more experience using the balance scale, have them more closely estimate weights of objects before they use the scale to measure them.

☆ Use more closely calibrated weights so children can weigh with greater accuracy.

☆ Weigh the same objects on a balance scale with fixed weights and then on a modern digital or spring scale. Discuss any variations children may notice.

Quickies

Build a Balance Scale

Don't despair if you don't have access to store-bought balance scales. There are several ways for children to make their own balance scales that will work for many weighing activities. For example, they can hang two paper cups from either end of the crossbar of a coat hanger, then hang the hook on a nail or doorknob. Or they can make a balance scale from a board and something that functions as a fulcrum, or they can attach plastic margarine or yogurt cups to the ends of a ruler and set the ruler on a fulcrum. Consult science books and your mathematics textbook for more specific directions.

Watery Weights

Water may not feel like much drop by drop, but it definitely has weight. Have children investigate the weights of objects when they are dry and when they are wet. For instance, they can weigh a dry sponge, then douse it with water and weigh it again. Or they can weigh a houseplant before and after watering it. They might place an ice cube in a paper cup and weigh it when it is solid and again when it melts. Use nonstandard or formal units as you see fit.

Corny Ideas

Does 1 cup of unpopped kernels weigh the same as 1 cup of popped popcorn? Which weighs the most: 1 cup of microwave popcorn, 1 cup of air-popped popcorn, or 1 cup of popcorn popped the old-fashioned way? Have children brainstorm other "popcorn questions" and ways to find the answers. Measure, pop, measure again, and then celebrate the findings by having a popcorn snack!

Create a Kilogram

What does a kilogram look like? What does it feel like? Help children fill a resealable plastic bag with sand, dirt, water, salt, rice, or dried beans until it weighs 1 kilogram. Have them compare this benchmark weight with weights of various classroom objects.

Stuffed Shoes

Just exactly how big is your shoe?

Children may know their official shoe size, but that's only one way to measure it. If they can envision a shoe as an oddly shaped container that can hold objects, they'll see that shoe size can be measured in more ways than one.

The Plan

1 Tell children that although some of them may have the same shoe size, it doesn't mean that their shoes are exactly the same size. In this activity, children will investigate the capacity of their shoe, or how much it can hold.

2 Prepare children by asking them to wear shoes—not sandals or boots—to school on the day of the activity. You might bring in some extra shoes, just in case.

3 Provide large quantities of objects to be used as units of capacity. Have children remove one shoe and fill it with as many of the units as possible.

4 When the shoe is full, have children empty its contents and count them. Record this number on a class chart.

5 Make a graph that compares children's shoes by capacity. If children used different objects, group those who used the same objects so the comparisons make sense.

6 As a variation, divide the class into groups. Group members select one or two shoes to fill. Groups then share their findings with the class to compare and contrast results.

> **MATERIALS**
> ☆ marbles, connecting cubes, unit cubes, peanuts in the shell, play coins, or any other small objects available in large quantity
> ☆ children's shoes
> ☆ chart paper
> ☆ markers

Follow-Up

☆ Try a variation of this activity by having children fill a pocket, their cupped hands, a change purse, and so on. Discuss any observations children make.

☆ Talk about the problems children encountered in this activity. What would make it work better another time? How do people actually measure how much something holds?

Hold It!

Can the same-size paper be rolled to make containers of two different sizes?

The dimensions of a container affect how much it holds. Even young children can grasp this concept with this simple, hands-on investigation.

The Plan

1 Divide the class into pairs. Give each pair two 9- x 12-inch sheets of construction paper (color doesn't matter). Have them roll each sheet into a tube in two different ways—a tall, thin tube (side to side) and a wide, short tube (top to bottom). Have them use masking tape to fasten the ends together so that the tube holds its shape, but make sure they do not overlap the ends too much—they want as large a tube as possible for the paper they use. Then have them tightly tape a cardboard square to form a base that will close off the bottom and allow the tube to stand up.

> **MATERIALS**
> ☆ 9- x 12-inch sheets of construction paper
> ☆ masking tape
> ☆ cardboard squares
> ☆ popcorn

2 Have children examine the two tubes and then guess which one holds more. Some children may guess that since the tubes were formed from same-size sheets of paper, they will hold the same amount. Others may guess that one tube or the other will hold more. Tally the guesses before children investigate.

3 Provide popcorn. Have children fill one tube to the top. Using that filled tube, they can pour it into the other tube to figure out whether it holds more, less, or the same amount of popcorn. (If pouring overflows the second tube, the first one is bigger.)

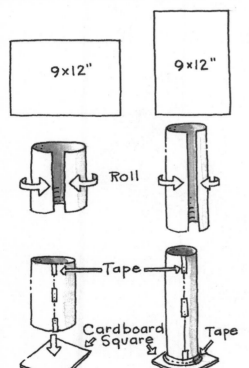

Follow-Up

☆ Repeat the activity with different sizes of paper.

☆ Discuss the results. Talk about why the same-size paper can form containers that hold different amounts. Guide children to conclude that the shape and size of a container affect how much it can hold.

Pouring Sand

How can you tell which container holds the most?

When containers have different shapes, even some adults aren't sure which holds the most. In this activity, children compare capacities in a hands-on way. This time, they use a standard measuring tool to help them.

The Plan

1 Talk with children about times when it helps to know how much a container can hold. Then show them some containers that are different sizes and shapes. Select ones with relatively similar capacities. Also make sure that none obviously holds a known capacity (such as liter pop bottles or 1-quart milk containers). Ask children to tell how they might figure out which container holds the most and which holds the least.

2 Divide the class into pairs or trios. Have children cover their work area with newspaper (to make subsequent cleanup easier). Give each group three different-sized plastic containers and a bucket of sand. Provide a measuring cup, a funnel, and a scoop for transferring sand. Review how to read a measuring cup, if necessary.

3 Have groups rank the three empty containers from smallest to largest just by looking at them. Have them number the containers 1 (smallest) to 3 (largest).

4 Then have children use the sand to figure out how much each container actually holds. Explain how to pour the sand back and forth between the container, the measuring cup, and the bucket to determine how much each container holds. Have children record this information and repeat for each container.

5 When children have measured all containers and have adjusted the ranking as necessary, have them put all the sand back into the bucket and clean up the work area.

> **MATERIALS**
> ☆ different-sized plastic containers
> ☆ buckets of sand
> ☆ old newspapers
> ☆ measuring cups
> ☆ funnels
> ☆ scoops
> ☆ chart paper
> ☆ pencils

Follow-Up

☆ How did group predictions compare with actual results?

☆ Repeat and extend by challenging groups to rank four or five different containers.

☆ Take the activity outside, and use water to test the capacity of containers.

Fill 'Er Up!

How good are you at estimating cupfuls?

Jars, jugs, bowls, and pitchers come in all shapes and sizes, which can be described in terms of the number of cups each contains. (A cup holds 8 fluid ounces.) In this activity, children estimate and then measure the capacity, in cups, of different large containers.

The Plan

1 Divide the class into small groups. Prepare a recording chart like this for each group:

Container	Estimate How Many Cups Fill It	Actual Number of Cups	Comments

2 Give each group an 8-ounce paper or plastic cup, a large container, a funnel (if necessary), and a pan to serve as a catch basin.

3 Have children examine and describe the big container. Then have them guess how many cups they think it will take to fill it. Have them record their guess and then check it by pouring cups of water into the large container.

4 Remind them to count and/or tally as they go and record the actual count.

5 Repeat with other large containers.

MATERIALS

☆ 8-ounce cups (paper or plastic)

☆ various large containers (pitchers, vases, empty soft-drink bottles, bowls, jugs, jars, and so on)

☆ funnels (optional)

☆ pans

☆ water

☆ paper towels or sponges

☆ recording chart (see above)

☆ pencils

Follow-Up

☆ Notice whether the ability to estimate improves with subsequent investigations.

☆ Use this activity to lead into a study of ounces, cups, pints, quarts, and gallons.

Follow the Liter

Can you tell how big a liter is?

Although Americans continue to use customary rather than metric units for most measures, the liter has become a familiar size in the U.S. marketplace. This activity helps children get a sense of the capacity of a liter.

The Plan

1 Display a 1-liter bottle. Ask children what kinds of things usually come in containers like this (liquids such as soda, milk, or juice).

2 Display an assortment of unlabeled bottles. Ask volunteers to try to select bottles that hold less than 1 liter, more than 1 liter, and about 1 liter.

3 Divide the class into groups. Give each group a 1-liter bottle, some unlabeled bottles (some greater, some less than 1 liter), and a catch basin. Have children pour water from the 1-liter bottle into the other containers to determine which ones hold more than 1 liter and which hold less than 1 liter. Provide funnels, if needed.

4 Then have children pour water from the 1-liter bottle into a paper cup to determine about how many servings of that size a 1-liter bottle would provide.

> **MATERIALS**
> ☆ labeled 1-liter bottles
> ☆ various unlabeled bottles that hold more and less than 1 liter
> ☆ catch basins
> ☆ water
> ☆ funnels (optional)
> ☆ paper cups
> ☆ paper towels or sponges

Follow-Up

☆ Knowing about how many servings are in a liter is a useful real-life fact. Plan a class party that involves beverages sold in 1-liter containers. Help children figure out how many liters to buy so that everyone in the class can have a paper cup serving.

☆ Conduct a similar investigation using quarts or gallons.

Equivalent Measures Match

Can you identify capacity measures that are expressed in different units?

Ounces, cups, pints, quarts, gallons—our customary measurement system demands that children learn the relationships among these units. This simple card game can help!

The Plan

1 Reproduce three sets of the cards on pages 36–37 and cut them apart.

2 The object of the game is to get the greatest number of equivalent pairs.

3 Set up groups of three to five players. Give each group a prepared, shuffled deck. Have one child deal out five cards to each player. The remaining cards go facedown in a pile.

4 In turn, players follow these rules:

☆ The "asker" asks the player to his or her left, "Do you have a match for _____?" and reads off the measure on the card he or she holds.

☆ If the "answerer" holds an equivalent measure, such as 8 ounces for 1 cup, he or she gets the asker's card. The answerer shows both cards to the group for confirmation of the match. Once the match is confirmed, the answerer puts both cards aside to be counted later.

☆ If the answerer cannot make a match, he or she says, "No match." The asker must draw a card from the facedown pile. Play moves to the next person.

☆ If an asker holds two cards that match, he or she can reveal them on any turn.

☆ Play continues until all matches have been made, or until someone runs out of cards. The winner is the player with the greatest number of equivalent measure matches.

> **MATERIALS**
> ☆ Equivalent Measures Match Cards (pages 36–37)
> ☆ display containers labeled 1 cup, 1 pint, 1 quart, $\frac{1}{2}$ gallon, and 1 gallon

LIQUID MEASURE KEY

8 ounces	=	1 cup	=	$\frac{1}{2}$ pint				
16 ounces	=	2 cups	=	1 pint	=	$\frac{1}{2}$ quart		
32 ounces	=	4 cups	=	2 pints	=	1 quart		
64 ounces	=	8 cups	=	4 pints	=	2 quarts	=	$\frac{1}{2}$ gallon
128 ounces	=	16 cups	=	8 pints	=	4 quarts	=	1 gallon

Follow-Up

☆ Vary the deck to include other kinds of measures.

☆ Use some of the same cards to play Equivalent Measures Concentration.

8 ounces	**16 ounces**
32 ounces	**64 ounces**
128 ounces	**1 cup**
2 cups	**4 cups**
8 cups	**16 cups**

$^1/_2$ **pint**	$^1/_2$ **quart**
$^1/_2$ **gallon**	**1 pint**
2 pints	**4 pints**
1 quart	**2 quarts**
4 quarts	**1 gallon**

Measurement Muffins & Capacity Cider

Can you apply your understanding of measures to make yummy treats?

Nothing reinforces the value of measuring better than following recipes. Here are two simple treats children can make in school (if you have access to an oven) or at home to practice working with units of capacity.

The Plan

1 If you have access to an oven in school, you can make the apple muffins together. The cider requires no cooking. Or send home the recipes so children can make them there with adult supervision.

2 Read the recipes together. Identify units of measure and the tools you need to measure ingredients. Work with children to determine how many batches of muffins and cider to make for everyone in the class. (Don't forget to include the teacher!)

3 Help children follow the steps of the recipes. Enjoy your snack together!

MATERIALS
☆ ingredients and utensils (page 39)
☆ copies of the recipes (page 39)
☆ napkins
☆ cups
☆ serving ladle
☆ materials for cleaning up

Follow-Up

☆ Help children use problem-solving skills to analyze the recipes. Pose the following questions:

How much applesauce would you need to make a double batch of muffins? How much honey? How much flour?

How much cider and seltzer would you need to make half a batch of fizzy cider?

Suppose you make 1 batch of muffins and you want to serve 1 cup of milk with each muffin. How much milk do you need?

☆ Have children contribute family recipes to a class cookbook of easy foods to make or bake. Focus on measurement units.

Apple Muffins & Fizzy Cider

Which do you prefer?

Ingredients for 12 Muffins		Utensils
1½ cups applesauce	1 tablespoon baking powder	mixing bowls and spoons
1 egg, lightly beaten	½ teaspoon baking soda	measuring cups and spoons
¼ cup honey or molasses	1 teaspoon cinnamon	muffin cups or greased muffin tin
5 teaspoons vegetable oil	½ cup raisins (optional)	pot holder
2 cups flour		

The Plan

1 Preheat oven to 375° F.

2 In one bowl, mix together the applesauce, egg, honey or molasses, and oil. Set aside.

3 In another bowl, combine the flour, baking powder, baking soda, and cinnamon.

4 Add applesauce mixture to flour mixture. Stir just enough to moisten. Add raisins, if desired.

5 Spoon batter into 12 muffin cups. Bake for 20 minutes. Cool and enjoy!

Ingredients for 12 Servings of Cider	Utensils
2 quarts apple cider	punch bowl or large pitcher
1 pint seltzer	measuring cups
½ cup cherries	mixing spoon

The Plan

1 In a punch bowl or large pitcher, combine the cider and seltzer.

2 Drain the cherries and add to the cider mix. Enjoy!

Quickies

Fluid Field Trip

It's one thing to study capacity in class; it's another to study capacity in the real world. Taking your class on a neighborhood field trip can help children gain a better appreciation for capacity measures. Make arrangements to visit a local supermarket or grocery store. Tell children that the purpose of the trip is to investigate the assortment of different-sized containers that hold beverages, cooking ingredients, cleaning fluids, and other kinds of liquids. Before the trip, prepare a "Fluid Field Trip Log" on which students can record their findings. The log can include three columns: one for the type of liquid, one for the container size, and one for comments. At the store, divide the class into groups and assign an adult to supervise each group. Have groups walk through the store collecting data.

Give Me a Hand

An ancient nonstandard unit of measure that is available to all of us is the handful. Do an activity in which children estimate and then figure out how many of various kinds of objects they can hold in one hand. Provide bowls of buttons, spools, connecting cubes, macaroni, crayons, peanuts, paper clips, jelly beans, and so on. First have children guess how much or how many of each object they could hold. Then have them try. Establish ground rules for all to follow, such as: Do you grab a handful or scoop it? Do you use one hand to fill the other? How do you determine when your hand is full? Provide a simple chart in which children can record their guess and the actual count. Discuss with children why this is a nonstandard unit of measurement.

Let It Pour!

Can children recognize 1 cup without a measuring cup at hand? Fill an unlabeled pitcher or bottle with water. Provide bowls or jars that are not standard 1-cup sizes but that can hold at least 1 cup. Challenge children to pour water from the bottle into the bowl or jar, stopping when they think they have poured 1 cup. Then transfer the poured water to a measuring cup to see how close the estimate was. Repeat to build children's visual/spatial sense of the capacity of 1 cup. Vary by pouring other quantities, such as 1 pint or 1 quart.

Have Your Fill

The carnival midway isn't the only place for contests! Have capacity estimation contests in your classroom each day. Each morning, display a different-sized container and some sample objects that might be used to fill the container. Have children guess how many of that particular object it will take to fill it. They can write their guesses, with their names, on a sheet of paper placed near the container. At the end of the day, fill the container with the objects to find out whose guess came the closest. Repeat often and vary the size of the container and the kinds of objects used to fill it.

Clock Collections

How can we learn to tell time when clocks look so different?

Clocks tell time, and they also reflect trends in fashion, design, and pop culture. An interactive bulletin board can help children focus on what all clocks and watches have in common.

The Plan

1 Divide the class into small groups. Provide each group with some old catalogs and magazines that they can look through to find pictures of clocks and watches. Have children cut out the images they find and paste them onto poster paper to present as their "clock collection."

2 Display the various clock collection posters on a bulletin board entitled "What Time Is It?" Challenge children to read the times on the clock faces.

3 Invite children to add other pictures of clocks and watches to the display whenever they come across them at home or in school.

> **MATERIALS**
> ☆ bulletin board space
> ☆ old catalogs and magazines
> ☆ scissors
> ☆ poster paper
> ☆ paste

Follow-Up

☆ Guide children to examine and analyze the collections. Ask questions such as these:

What features do all (or most of) the clocks and watches share?

What characteristics can you find to sort the clocks?

Do any of the clocks tell the same time?

Which clocks are hardest to read? Which are the easiest?

Which clocks do you like best? Which do you like least?

☆ Have children use self-sticking notes to write the time and attach the notes near the clocks of their choice.

☆ Have a class clock show-and-tell. Invite children to bring in a clock or watch from home and talk about it with classmates.

How Long Is a Minute?

Do you know how long a minute really lasts?

A minute can feel like an eternity (think headache!) or fly by in a flash (think roller coaster!). This activity will help children build time sense.

The Plan

1 Ask children to think of things that last a minute. Record their suggestions on the chalkboard. Then ask children if they know how long a minute really is. Some will be able to say that a minute is 60 seconds. Challenge them to explain how long that is!

> **MATERIALS**
> ☆ watch or clock with second hand

2 Tell children that you are going to see how well they can sense when 1 minute has gone by. Have them put their heads down and close their eyes. Tell them that after you say "Start!" they should imagine a minute passing by. When they think a minute has passed, have them raise their hands, keeping their eyes closed. As hands go up, jot down names and times, if you can. (It helps to have a prepared list of names.)

3 When a minute is up, say "Stop." Identify children who felt the minute went by too quickly and those who didn't think that a minute had passed. Invite children to share what they think helped them to sense when a minute had passed.

4 Repeat the activity several times to help children improve their "minute sense."

Follow-Up

☆ Vary the task by playing music, turning the lights out, having children do some kind of simple activity (such as reading or drawing), and so on.

☆ Vary the signaling method by having children start out standing. Have them sit when they think that a minute has passed.

☆ Share time-honored tricks of counting by seconds, such as saying "1-Mississippi, 2-Mississippi, 3-Mississippi…" and so on. Some people say "mashed potatoes" after every number while they count so that they don't count too fast. Invite children to ask adults they know to share their own tricks.

Activities That Take...

How long do familiar activities usually take?

To continue to build time sense, ask children to think about how long familiar activities typically take.

The Plan

> **MATERIALS**
> ☆ clock or watch
> ☆ class schedule (optional)
> ☆ recording chart (see below)
> ☆ pencils

① Divide the class into small groups. Provide each group with a recording chart, like the one shown here, on which children can list activities that take each amount of time:

About 1 Minute	About 5 Minutes	About 15 Minutes	About 1/2 Hour	About 1 Hour

② Have children work together to fill in at least five examples in each time category. Guide them to consider daily routines such as brushing teeth, walking the dog, packing lunch, getting to school, doing certain household or school chores, and so on. Encourage children to be creative. It might help them to consult a clock, watch, or class schedule to spark ideas. As needed, suggest benchmark times with which children can compare their ideas. Tell them, for example, that snack time is 15 minutes.

③ Bring groups together to share their lists. Encourage discussion as you compile a class chart. If some time categories are under-represented, provide hints to help children add to the chart.

Follow-Up

☆ Extend the activity to include longer times, such as 1 day, 1 week, 1 month, or 1 year, or time ranges such as 2–4 hours, 6–8 hours, 12–16 hours, and so on.

☆ Designate a day during which you guide children to pay attention to how long things really do take. They may be quite surprised!

Living Clock

Can you tell time when you are part of the clock itself?

Kinesthetic learners will revel in this activity that helps everyone practice telling time on the analog clock.

The Plan

1 Before class, prepare a set of large number cards (1–12). Punch two holes at the tops of the cards, through which you loop yarn so that children can wear the cards on their chests.

2 Mix the cards, hand them out at random to 12 children, and ask them to put on the numbers. Have these children order themselves in a circle so that they represent the numbers on the face of an analog clock. Have them hold hands so they stay in a circular formation, like the numbers around the clock face.

3 Choose someone to be the clock's hands. Give that child two pointers of different lengths: the longer one to represent the minute hand, the shorter one for the hour hand.

4 Help "Hands" find the center of the circle. Then have "Hands" think of a time and show it on the human clock by directing the pointers toward the appropriate numbers on the "clock face" (or between them, depending on the time). The other children guess what time the human clock shows. Allow one child who gives the correct time to take over as the new "Hands." Continue until everyone has had a chance to participate. Have a new group of students take over as the clock numbers so that everyone has a chance to be both a number and "Hands."

> **MATERIALS**
> ☆ large number cards 1–12
> ☆ hole punch
> ☆ yarn
> ☆ yardstick or meter stick
> ☆ inch or centimeter ruler (or dowels or sticks of two lengths to serve as clock hands)

Follow-Up

☆ Form two human clocks. Display a time written in digital form. Have the "Hands" of both clocks show that time.

☆ Use the human clock formation to practice counting by fives. Have a volunteer walk around the outside of the circle, tapping each number on the head as the class counts together.

Time Concentration

Can you match times that are presented in analog and in digital form?

Nowadays, the ubiquitous digital clock has made some children less familiar with telling time on the analog clock. This activity can help bridge that gap.

The Plan

1 Before class, prepare play decks of cards that show times in both analog form (on a round clock face) and digital form. (If desired, reproduce the clock face below and glue it to cards.) Make 12–25 pairs of cards, showing times that fit the skill level of your class: times to the hour, half-hour, and quarter-hour, or times to the minute.

MATERIALS
☆ index cards
☆ marker
☆ analog clock (optional, see below)

2 Divide the class into small groups of three to five students. Give each group a playing deck. One child shuffles the deck and deals out all the cards facedown in rows for a variation on the old favorite, Concentration. The object of the game is to make as many matches as possible.

3 To play, players take turns flipping over any two cards and reading the times they show. If the cards match—an analog clock tells the same time as a digital clock—the player takes those cards and gets another turn. If cards do not match, the player turns them back over in their places and the next player's turn begins.

4 In this game, as in any variation of Concentration, all players must watch carefully as cards are revealed in order to remember where potential matches lie.

5 The game ends when all matches have been made. The player who has the most matches wins.

Follow-Up

☆ Vary the size of the deck and the times shown on the cards.

☆ Vary the deck by including pairs of word names that express the same times, such as "four forty-five" and "quarter to five," or "half-past seven" and "seven-thirty."

Day of Your Dreams

How would you spend your time if you were in total charge of your day?

Children and adults alike often long for "free time" that they can spend as they wish. In this activity, children get to plan their ideal day.

The Plan

① Ask children to imagine that they have the chance to spend a whole day—from the moment they wake up until bedtime—doing only what they would like. Give them time to think about this and ask them to jot down some things they'd want to do. Encourage them to be creative by telling them that they could be anywhere in the world on this day and with anyone they choose.

> **MATERIALS**
> ☆ schedule (see below)
> ☆ clock or watch

② Provide each child with a schedule such as the one below. Go over it with children to be sure that they understand their task—to list all activities they would do during this imaginary day, starting from whenever they decide to get up and filling the day until whatever bedtime they choose.

Morning		Afternoon		Evening	
Starting Time	Activity	Starting Time	Activity	Starting Time	Activity

③ After children have planned their ideal day's schedule, have them imagine the day and then make any revisions that seem necessary. Be sure they present their activities in sequential order—from reveille to taps!

Follow-Up

☆ Have children share and talk about their ideal day in small groups or as a whole class. Guide them to look for patterns, similarities, differences, omissions, and so on.

☆ Add a column labeled "Duration" to the chart. In this column, have children list the total amount of time they have allotted for each activity.

☆ Challenge children to summarize their ideal day by figuring out how much time they would have between wake-up time and bedtime.

Cuckoo Clocks

Can you read a clock without numbers? What happens if the power goes out?

It's one thing to be able to tell time. It's quite another to apply problem-solving skills to figure out the time when something's off—like the numbers or the electricity!

The Plan

1 Duplicate the reproducible and distribute a copy to each child or pair of children. Explain that this activity has two parts.

2 In Part 1, the clock faces have no numbers to help children read the times. Challenge children to write the times in the spaces given.

3 In Part 2, each digital clock shows a time when the power went off—so the clock stopped telling time. Challenge children to use the information given to figure out what time the clock should show. Provide demonstration clocks or watches that children can use to help them solve these "timely" problems.

Follow-Up

☆ Extend by creating similar "timely" problems for children to solve. If children can tell time to the minute, you can make the situations more challenging.

☆ Ask children to determine a bedtime. Then ask them to decide how many hours of sleep they would like to get. Have them figure out what time they will need to set their alarm clock to go off in the morning. Repeat this problem-solving activity by having students vary their bedtimes and sleeping durations.

Name: _____

Cuckoo Clocks

Part 1: No Numbers!

What time is it?

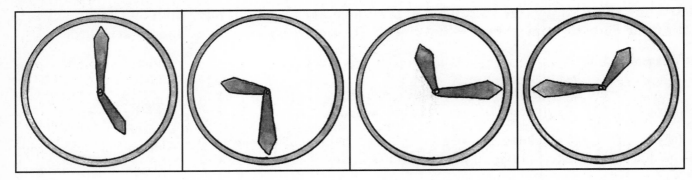

_____ _____ _____ _____

Part 2: No Power!

The power went off and so did the clocks! Figure out the real time.

2:40	Power was off for 30 minutes. What time should it show?_____
12:05	Power was off for 2 hours. What time should it show?_____
3:20	Power was off for 1 ½ hours. What time should it show?_____
8:37	Power was off for 59 minutes. What time should it show?_____

Class Calendar

How can you make a calendar that's just for you?

Groundhog Day, Presidents' Day, Independence Day—they're on most calendars. But what special dates would your students mark on a calendar that they created?

The Plan

1 Display the calendar for this month. Point to the first day of the month and ask children to tell what day it falls on. Have them identify the last day of the month, too. Ask them to name any holidays or special days the calendar shows.

MATERIALS
☆ current calendar
☆ calendar form (page 50)
☆ markers
☆ almanacs
☆ stickers (optional)

2 Divide the class into 12 groups. Assign each group a different month of the year. (Divide a smaller class into six groups and assign each group two months.) Then give each group a blank calendar form. Have them use the current year's calendar to determine on which day of the week the month begins and how many days the month has. Then have them fill out the grid by correctly numbering the days. (Guide them to write numbers fairly small in a corner of the boxes; they'll need room to write more information in some cells.)

3 Have groups list their month's important dates. They may have to consult an almanac or other resource for help. Then invite them to lengthen the list by including birthdays of friends and family members, special days (such as the date they got their pet), and days of events of interest to them, their family, the school, or the community. Then have groups use their lists to highlight these important dates on their calendars. They can add stickers, small pictures, or words, as appropriate.

4 Invite groups to present their personalized calendars to classmates. Have them describe the calendar's interesting features.

Follow-Up

☆ Combine all the monthly calendars to form a personalized class calendar for the year. Invite children to add to it as the year progresses and new special events come up.

Class Calendar

How can you make a calendar that's just for you?

Month _____

Sunday	Monday	Tuesday	Wednesday	Thursday	Friday	Saturday

Timely Arrival

How can you ensure that a birthday card you mail will arrive on time?

When we send a birthday card, we want it to get there on time. Although mail delivery can sometimes be unpredictable, children can determine when to mail cards by using a rule-of-thumb and counting backward on a calendar.

MATERIALS
☆ current calendar
☆ recording table (see below)
☆ pencils

The Plan

1 Distribute copies of a table like the one shown. This table includes a sample row.

Person With Birthday	Month and Date of Birthday	Day of Birthday	Date to Mail Card	Day to Mail Card
Marcia	January 9	Monday	January 5	Thursday

2 Have children choose five people to whom they might send birthday cards this year. Ask them to write those names on the table, followed by the date of each person's birthday. Then have them use this year's calendar to find the days of the week on which the birthdays fall. Ask them to add those dates to the table.

3 Tell children that if they want a letter to arrive by a certain date, they should mail it three days ahead of time. Mail isn't delivered on Sunday or on major holidays, so they have to skip these days as they are counting. Point out that if a birthday falls on Sunday or on one of those holidays, children should plan to have the cards arrive a day earlier.

4 Ask children to follow the above guidelines to complete the last two columns of the table—the date and day to mail each card. They can use calendars to count backward to determine this information.

Follow-Up

☆ Have children interview a letter carrier to find out exactly what happens to a letter from the time it goes into a mailbox to when it reaches its destination.

Wacky Holiday Watch

When do wacky holidays fall?

Children may know that some holidays, like Valentine's Day (February 14), always fall on the same date; the dates of others, like Mother's Day (second Sunday in May), change from year to year. Do any of your students know that National Juggling Day is always June 19, but that the dates of Stagecoach Days vary from year to year?

The Plan

1 Distribute copies of this year's calendar to pairs of children. Discuss the idea that some holidays always occur on the same date, whereas others are always celebrated on the same day of the week but may fall on a different date from year to year. Tell them, for instance, that we always honor veterans on November 11, no matter what day of the week it falls on. By contrast, Father's Day is always the third Sunday in June, whatever the date. Have children identify the day of the week for Veteran's Day and the date of Father's Day this year.

> **MATERIALS**
> ☆ current calendar

2 Invite children to identify other holidays that always fall on the same date or that always fall on the same day.

3 Present the following list of lesser-known holidays. Ask children to figure out the date or dates on which each will fall this year.

- ☆ **National Grandparent's Day**— the first Sunday in September following Labor Day

- ☆ **Chocolate Festival**—the Saturday before Valentine's Day

- ☆ **Be Kind to Animals Week**— the first full week of May

- ☆ **National Teacher Day**—the Tuesday of the first full week of May

- ☆ **Donut Days**—the first Friday and Saturday in June

Follow-Up

☆ Challenge children to figure out the earliest and latest date that each of the above holidays could fall on in any given year.

☆ Invite children to come up with the dates of other unusual holidays. One source of information they can use is Scholastic's *Every Day of the School Year Math Problems* by Marcia Miller and Martin Lee.

Quickies

Time for Fun

What activities do children enjoy doing the most? Is it eating ice cream? Swimming? Playing with their pet? When do they ordinarily get to do these things? To find out, draw several clocks without hands on a sheet of paper and make a copy for each child. Next, ask children to write the name of the fun activity above the clock and then to draw the hands of the clock showing the time when they are most likely to be doing that activity.

What Time Is It?

During the course of a day, children, just like grown-ups, often want to know the time. They might want to know how much longer until lunch, how long they'll have to wait before a movie starts, or for how much longer they'll be allowed to stay up. About how often do they check the time? First ask them to guess. Then, to get a more accurate estimate, have them create recording sheets on which to list the times they check the time in one column, and whatever they were doing at that time in the other. Children can have these sheets with them all day, starting from when they first awaken and look at the clock, right up until they go to sleep. As they check the time, they record it and briefly write why they wanted to know it. On the next day, have children compare their findings.

Calendar Riddles

Present the following two riddles to children:

☆ "It's Monday, January 9. What is the date three Tuesdays from now?" (January 24)

☆ "In May, the 29th was a Thursday. On what day did the 29th of April fall?" (Tuesday)

Challenge children to create their own calendar riddles for classmates to solve. Compile them in a binder that children can look through and pick from when they have free time.

Time Over Time

Tell children that various cultures have come up with different ways to tell time. If possible, show pictures or actual examples of some of these. You might choose to display a sundial, an hourglass, an Egyptian water clock or shadow clock, or a Japanese lantern clock. Invite children to examine and draw them. Talk about how they work.

Measurement Tool Tally

What measurement tools do you have in your house?

Your classroom is probably bursting with measuring tools: rulers, tape measures, balance scales, measuring cups, thermometers, clocks, and probably some wristwatches. But to find a greater breadth of measuring tools, there's no place like home. Children will be surprised at how many measurement tools they'll find around their house.

The Plan

1 Tell children that they are going to survey how many measurement tools they have around their homes. Review how to make tally marks.

2 Begin by brainstorming with children the many kinds of measuring devices, from calendars to tape measures, that they might find at home. Remind them to count tools like fish tank thermometers and timers on VCRs.

> **MATERIALS**
> ☆ Tool Tally table (see below)
> ☆ pencils

3 Provide children with a table, like the one started here, that they can use to record their findings. Encourage them to add to it as they uncover different types of devices.

Measuring Tool	Tally	Total
Clock		
Watch		
Scale		
Ruler		

4 Have children take their tally tables home and work with family members to fill them in. The next day, have them compare findings with those of classmates. Are there any surprises?

Follow-Up

☆ Have children first guess and then find the total number of different kinds of measuring tools the class found at home.

☆ Do a measurement tool tally in your classroom and in other school rooms, if possible.

Measure Match

Which tool will you choose?

You can create an interactive bulletin board to help children review which measuring tools are used to measure which kinds of objects.

The Plan

1 Make a large three-section bulletin board display entitled "Measuring Tools." Place a picture of a ruler at the top of the first section, a picture of a scale at the top of the middle section, and one of a liquid measuring cup at the top of the last section.

2 Have children search through old magazines, catalogs, and newspapers for pictures of things that could be measured by one of these tools. Ask them to cut out the pictures and place them in the envelope.

> **MATERIALS**
> ☆ old magazines, catalogs, and newspapers
> ☆ scissors
> ☆ tacks
> ☆ large manila envelope

3 Invite volunteers, in turn, to reach into the envelope and pull out one picture. Challenge them to tack the picture in the column with the measuring tool most suited to the object the picture shows. Ask them to explain why they selected that tool. Continue until the bulletin board is full of pictures.

Follow-Up

☆ Ask children to explain what the objects in each section of the bulletin board display have in common.

☆ Challenge children to draw pictures of objects to add to each column. (Encourage them to draw objects that are not already included on the display.)

☆ Have older children write measurement words on index cards and tack them up in the appropriate column. Examples: *pound, gallon, centimeter,* and so on.

Measurement Scavenger Hunt

What classroom objects of given measurements can you find?

Children can sharpen their skills in estimating and in visual/spatial reasoning as they find objects based on measurements. You can also use this activity as an informal assessment—by watching children work, you can determine which measuring skills they need more help to learn.

The Plan

1 Prepare a checklist of items children will hunt for in the classroom. Describe each item in terms of a measurement unit. Include length, perimeter, area, weight, time, and capacity. For example, you might ask them to find the following:

☆ a book that weighs more than 2 pounds

☆ a pencil 4–6 inches long

☆ a picture with a perimeter of about 30 inches

☆ a child taller than 4 $\frac{1}{2}$ feet

☆ a container that holds more than 1 quart but less than 1 gallon

☆ a non-digital watch

> ### MATERIALS
> ☆ scavenger hunt checklist (see Step 1)
> ☆ various measuring tools
> ☆ pencils

2 Go over the scavenger hunt rules. Decide whether you want children to actually collect the items or simply identify and describe them. Decide whether to set a time limit. Then determine how and when to verify measurements.

3 Distribute checklists to individuals or to small groups. Make sure that everyone has access to measurement tools. Then conduct the hunt according to the rules you've established.

4 When the hunt is over, provide time for children to tell how they found, estimated, and measured the items on the list.

Follow-Up

☆ Have children work with family members on another scavenger hunt at home. Invite them to use the same checklist or to make up their own.

☆ Hold another measurement scavenger hunt outdoors.

Too-Tall Tales

How can you recognize a far-fetched measurement tale?

It's usually easy enough to recognize a tall tale when you hear one. How easy is it for children to spot a "fishy story" when they hear one? Is it as easy for them to make one up?

The Plan

1 Tell children that you know someone who caught a fish that weighed 5,000 pounds. Ask them what they think about this. Then explain that the measurement data you provided is not believable. Ask a volunteer to retell your story, replacing the outlandish number with a sensible one. For example, children might say that the fish weighed 5 pounds. Repeat with another story, such as one that uses time or capacity measures.

2 Next, have children create several of their own measurement tall-tale stories. Make sure they know to include data that's either much too long, too short, too heavy, too light, too big, or too small.

3 Then have children form groups. Invite them to take turns presenting their stories to the group. After each child tells a story, others in the group must correct it by supplying reasonable measurement data.

4 Invite groups to share some of the funnier or most unbelievable stories.

Follow-Up

☆ Challenge children to find an article in a magazine or newspaper and then change any measurements included to make the article into a tall tale.

Measurement Marathon

How can you use your measurement skills in a class contest?

Now that children have spent time exploring and working with different kinds of measurement, it's time to summarize and celebrate their new skills.

The Plan

1 Ask children what multi-event sports contests they know, such as your school's field day or the Olympics. Explain that these contests include a variety of events.

2 Plan a Measurement Marathon with your class. Explain that it will involve six fun measuring events: Count Crunch (time), Extreme Mini-Golf (length), Perimeter Pursuit (perimeter), Balance Battle (weight), Cup Rush (capacity), and Calendar Setup (time). Each event is briefly described on the next page. Feel free to make adjustments. For instance, change a time limit, vary a rule, or let kids participate in pairs.

3 In advance, discuss the rules and procedures everyone will follow. For example, how many events can a child try? Will there be practice time before the actual contest? Will there be teams? Who will be judges, timers, and scorekeepers? How will you arrange the classroom? Who will gather, set up, and clean up materials? Will you present awards?

4 Children can play individually, in pairs, or in teams. You may choose to hold individual contests or single-elimination tournaments. There can be one winner or many winners for each event.

5 Have fun!

> ### MATERIALS
> ☆ various materials (see page 59)
> ☆ award ribbons and participation stickers (optional)

Follow-Up

☆ Repeat any or all of these events from time to time to increase children's skills with measuring.

☆ Have your class sponsor a Measurement Marathon for a family math night.

Measurement Marathon— The Events

How can you resist these events?

Count Crunch

Materials: Stopwatch or clock with second hand

Object: Count from 1–100 as fast as possible.

Rules: Players must say each number so judge can hear it. Judge times the counting.

Winner: The person who counts the fastest wins.

Extreme Mini-Golf

Materials: Cotton balls, plastic spoons, tape measure

Object: "Drive" a cotton ball off a "tee" (starting spot) with a spoon "club."

Rules: Players get two tries, taking the longer distance. Judge measures distances.

Winner: The person whose cotton golf ball travels the farthest wins.

Perimeter Pursuit

Materials: Grid paper, pencil, straightedge

Object: Draw as many four-sided figures as possible that have a given perimeter.

Rules: Players have a two-minute time limit. No repeated figures. Judge counts all "legal" perimeters and disqualifies repeats or errors.

Winner: The person who draws the greatest number of figures in the given time wins.

Balance Battle

Materials: 2 balance scales, sand, 2 scoops, 8-ounce weight

Object: Measure out 8 ounces of sand on a balance scale.

Rules: Players start, scoop, and stop when pans balance. Judge verifies balance.

Winner: The person who balances the scale first wins.

Cup Rush

Materials: large bowl of water, medicine droppers, paper cups, measuring cup

Object: Estimate to fill a paper cup with 4 ounces of water.

Rules: Players use a medicine dropper to transfer water, stopping when they think the cup holds 4 ounces. Judge measures to verify capacity.

Winner: The person who comes closest to 4 ounces wins.

Calendar Setup

Materials: blank calendar form, tiles numbered 1–31, cards labeled Sunday–Saturday

Object: Unscramble and arrange parts of a calendar.

Rules: Players must position each day and number correctly so that the completed calendar matches the current month's calendar. Judge verifies accuracy.

Winner: The first person to set up his or her calendar correctly wins.

Measures Crossword Puzzle

Can you solve measurement clues to complete a crossword puzzle?

Here's one way for children to review the relationships among customary units of measure.

The Plan

1 Give each child a set of the Measures Puzzle reproducibles. (Page 61 is the puzzle grid, and page 62 provides the clues.)

2 Review how to solve a crossword puzzle. Remind children that each box in the grid holds one letter. Some words go across (left to right), while others go down (top to bottom). Be sure children understand that any word they enter into the puzzle grid must fit its clue *exactly*—the answer must make sense when you read it in its position within the clue.

3 Have children work with partners to solve the puzzle. Allow them to consult a dictionary or math book to check spelling, if necessary. You may want to post a complete word list in alphabetical order that children can consult for hints.

Follow-Up

☆ Challenge children to create their own simple crossword puzzles for classmates to solve.

☆ Work together with children to create a set of measurement clues, like the ones presented in the puzzle, that they can use to quiz each other.

Name _____

Measures Crossword Puzzle Grid

The Directions

All the clues in this puzzle are about customary measure. Check your spelling!

Name _____

Measures Crossword Puzzle Clues

Across

2. A _____ clock tells time only with numbers.

6. 32 ounces = 1 _____

8. 4 quarts = 1 _____

9. 8 ounces = 1 _____

11. A yard has 3 _____.

14. To _____ myself, I stand on a scale.

15. A _____ tells how heavy something is.

18. 1 minute = 60 _____

20. A _____ shows what time it is.

21. 1 _____ = 60 minutes

24. The abbreviation for *minute* is _____.

26. Falling _____ in an hourglass shows time passing.

27. A basketball player may be 7 feet _____.

28. The space inside a shape is its _____.

30. Use a _____ to measure length.

31. One quart has _____ cups.

32. _____ tells how far around a shape.

33. _____ is the abbreviation for the shortest month of the year.

Down

1. 2 _____ = 1 quart

3. 12 _____ = 1 foot

4. *Length* is how _____ something is.

5. 8 _____ = 1 cup

7. January is the first _____ of the year.

10. 16 ounces = 1 _____

12. A week has _____ days.

13. _____ means how wide something is.

14. Monday is the first day of a school _____.

16. A _____ shows months and dates.

17. 36 inches = 1 _____

19. Another name for 12:00 P.M. is _____.

22. Fifty-two weeks make _____ year.

23. 100 years = 1 _____.

24. Use _____ to measure distances between towns.

25. 365 days = 1 _____

26. We measure area in _____ units.

29. One yard has _____ feet.

31. *Distance* means how _____.

50 Fabulous Measurement Activities Scholastic Professional Books

Fun Facts

PART 1: Length/Perimeter/Area

☆ Hans Langseth of Norway had the world's longest beard. It measured 17 $^1/_2$ feet!

☆ The longest known snake, a reticulated python, was 32 feet 9 $^1/_2$ inches long!

☆ The tallest living tree is a redwood in Oregon. It towers over 365 feet high!

☆ The largest gingerbread house ever built measured 128 feet around the outside!

☆ The largest roof in the world (in Germany) has an area of 914,940 square feet!

PART 2: Weight

☆ Lucia Zarate (1863–1889) was the lightest known adult. She weighed 13 pounds!

☆ The heaviest animal was a female blue whale that measured 190 tons (380,000 pounds)!

☆ The lightest drive-able car can go 15 miles per hour. It weighs only 21 pounds!

☆ The world's largest coin was made in India in 1613. It weighed 32 pounds!

☆ The heaviest watermelon ever weighed in at 262 pounds!

PART 3: Capacity

☆ The most powerful fire engine can pump over 20,000 gallons of foam in 1 minute!

☆ On August 25, 1992, Joseph Love of Kenya milked 30 cows for 117 gallons of milk!

☆ The world's largest trash can holds 11,493 gallons of yucky throwaway stuff!

PART 4: Time

☆ Steve Woodmore of England spoke over 600 words in 1 minute!

☆ A creosote plant found in California is the oldest living plant—about 11,700 years old!

☆ Awazu, Japan, has the oldest known hotel. It opened in the year 717!

☆ In 1994, Ron Bower went around the world in a helicopter faster than anyone had ever done this. It took him 24 days, 4 hours, 36 minutes, and 24 seconds!

☆ On April 30, 1998, the Yankees and the Orioles played the longest 9-inning baseball game ever—4 hours and 21 minutes long! (The Yankees won 13-10.)

PART 5: Measurement Miscellany

☆ Amresh Kumar Jha of India balanced on one foot for 71 hours and 40 minutes!

☆ The world's smallest adult dog, a Yorkie, weighed 17 ounces on its first birthday!

☆ The largest bagel ever made weighed 563 pounds!

☆ The longest paper chain ever made was just over 37 miles long!

☆ The longest measured green bean grew to 48 inches in length!

Related Books

PART 1: Length/Perimeter/Area

☆ *Farmer Mack Measures His Pig* by Tony Johnston

☆ *George Shrinks* by William Joyce

☆ *How Big Is a Foot?* by Rolf Myller

☆ *How Tall Are You?* by JoAnne Nelson

☆ *Inch by Inch* by Leo Lionni

☆ *Much Bigger Than Martin* by Steven Kellogg

☆ *Supergrandpa* by David M. Schwartz

PART 2: Weight

☆ *How Much and How Many* by Jeanne Bendick

☆ *One-Eyed Jake* by Pat Hutchins

☆ *The Story of Ferdinand* by Munro Leaf

☆ *The Turnip: An Old Russian Folktale* by Katherine Milhous and Alice Dalgiesh

☆ *Weighing and Balancing* by Jane Srivastava

☆ *Who Sank the Boat?* by Pamela Allen

PART 3: Capacity

☆ *Carrot Holes and Frisbee Trees* by N. M. Bodecker

☆ *A House for Hermit Crab* by Eric Carle

☆ *Jam* by Margaret Mahy

☆ *Knowabout: Capacity* by Henry Pluckrose

☆ *The Mitten: A Ukranian Folktale* by Jan Brett

☆ *Spaces, Shapes, and Sizes* by Jane Srivastava

☆ *Teddy Bears' Picnic Cookbook* by Abigail Darling and Alexandra Day

PART 4: Time

☆ *All in a Day* by Mitsumasa Anno

☆ *The Best Time of Day* by Valerie Flournoy

☆ *Big Book of Time* by William Edmonds

☆ *Chicken Soup With Rice* by Maurice Sendak

☆ *Clocks and More Clocks* by Pat Hutchins

☆ *How Long? To Go, To Grow, To Know* by Ross Olney & Patricia Olney

☆ *My First Book of Time* by Claire Llewellyn

☆ *Nine O'Clock Lullaby* by Marilyn Singer

☆ *The Sun's Day* by Mordicai Gerstein

☆ *Thunder Cake* by Patricia Polacco

PART 5: Measurement Miscellany

☆ *Animal Superstars: Biggest, Strongest, Fastest, Smartest* by Russell Freedman

☆ *The Biggest, Smallest, Fastest, Tallest Things You've Ever Heard Of* by Robert Lopshire

☆ *Size: The Measure of Things* by Eric Laithwaite

☆ *Super, Super, Superwords* by Bruce McMillan

☆ *Take Me to Your Liter: Science and Math Jokes* by Charles Keller